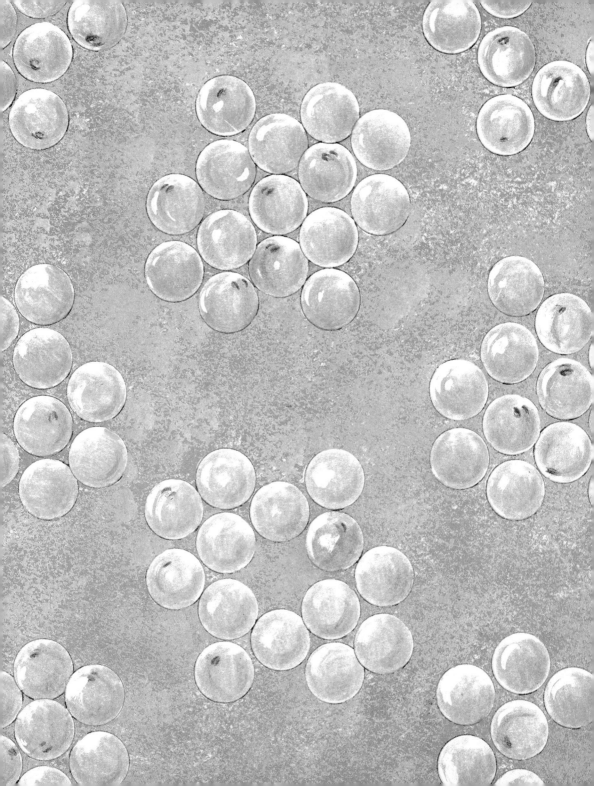

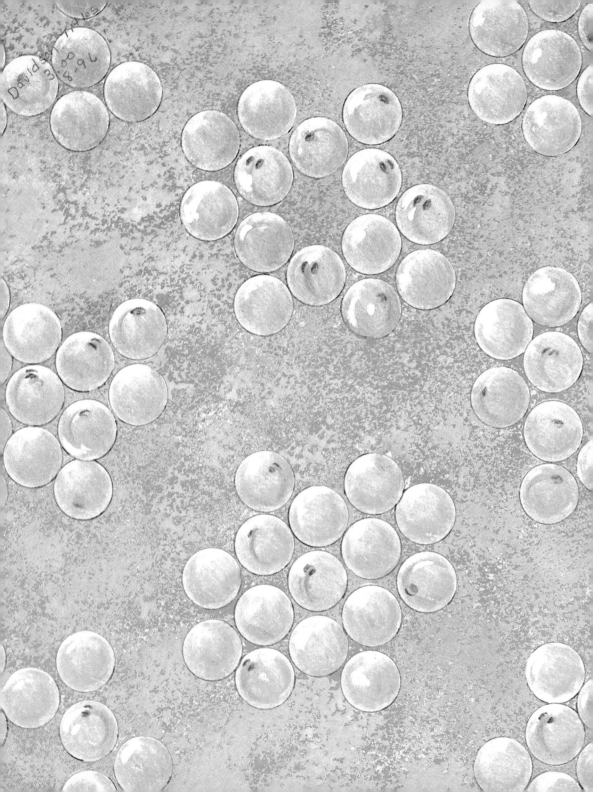

# FISH

designed and written by Althea
illustrated by Paul Wrigley

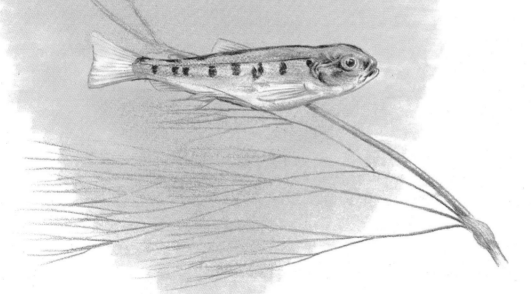

Longman Group USA Inc.

Published in the United States of America by Longman Group USA Inc.
© 1983, 1988 Althea Braithwaite

Originally published in Great Britain in a slightly altered form by Longman Group UK Limited

ISBN: 0-88462-182-0   (library bound)
ISBN: 0-88462-183-9   (paperback)

Printed in the United States of America

88  89  90  10  9  8  7  6  5  4  3  2  1

**Library of Congress Cataloging-in-Publication Data**

Althea.
   Fish / designed and written by Althea ; illustrated by Paul Wrigley.
   p.   cm.--(Life-cycle books / Althea)
   Summary: Describes the life cycle of the salmon, how it swims upstream to lay eggs, the hatching of the eggs, and how salmon find food.
   1. Salmon--Juvenile literature. [1. Salmon] I. Wrigley, Paul, ill. II. Title. III. Series: Althea. Life-cycle books.
QL638.S2A37  1988
597'.55--dc19                                        88-8507
ISBN 0-88462-182-0 (lib. bdg.)                       CIP
ISBN 0-88462-183-9 (pbk.)                            AC

**Notes for parents and teachers**
*Life-Cycle Books* have been specially written and designed as a simple, yet informative, series of factual nature books for young children.

The illustrations are bright and clear, and children can "read" the pictures while the story is read to them.

The text has been specially set in large type to make it easy for children to follow along or even to read for themselves.

The salmon has been
swimming and feeding
in cold ocean waters.
Now it is time for it to
swim the long way
back to the river
where it was born.

The salmon reach the coast
and start their long and
difficult journey
up the river.

The fish leap up waterfalls.
Exhausted, they rest,
then fight on against
the water as it rushes
down the river.

A male and female fish meet
and find a clean, clear pool.

The female's body is heavy with eggs.
She looks for a place to nest.

Flapping her tail
she turns from side to side,
moving the stones
to make her nest.

The male salmon keeps watch
to chase other males away.

The female lays thousands
of very small eggs.
The male fish swims
over the eggs and
fertilizes them
so that they will hatch.

In a week or two, the eggs
are all laid.
The female fish covers the nest
with small stones to protect
the eggs from being eaten
by enemies.

Now the fish leave the eggs.
They drift slowly down the river
and back to the ocean.

The eggs stay safely buried
at the bottom of the river
all through the winter.

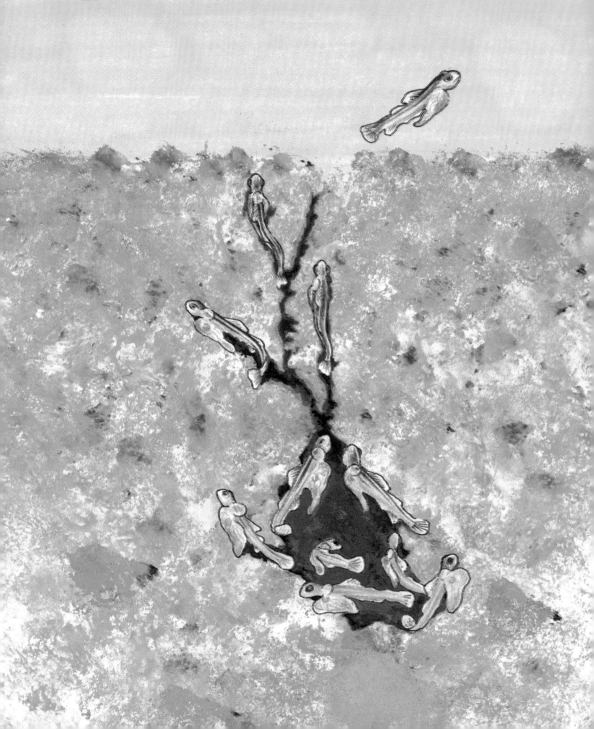

Spring arrives.
The tiny salmon hatch out.

At first each little fish
uses food from a yolk sac
attached to its body.
This was part of the egg
that held the fish before
it hatched.

After a few weeks
the small salmon wriggle
upward through the stones
to find food for themselves.

As the tiny salmon
hunt for their food,
many will get eaten
by larger fish or by birds.

When winter comes
the young salmon
that cannot find food
rest and sleep hidden
under the stones.

They grow slowly
each year.

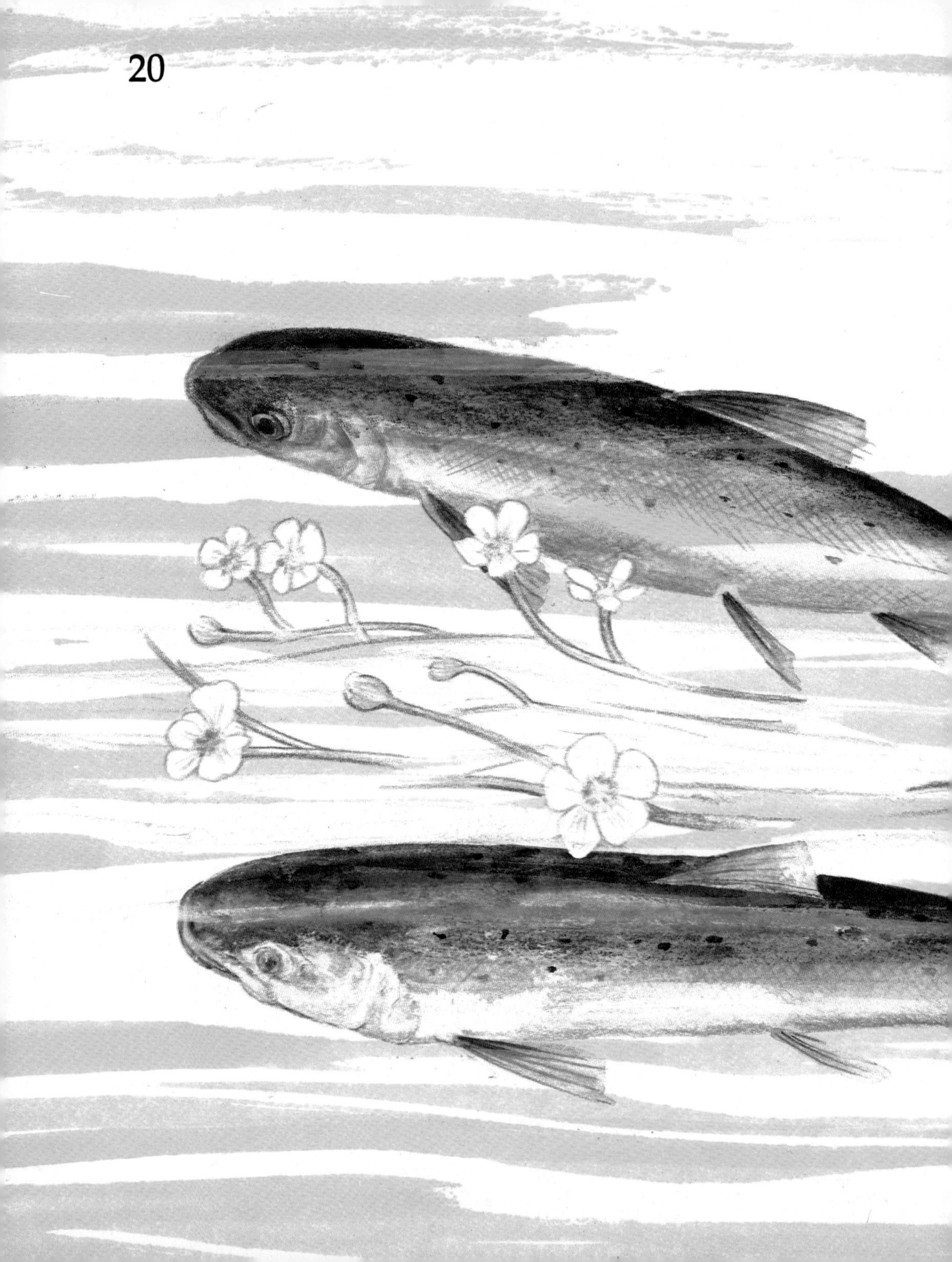

After one or two years,
it is time for the fish
to swim down the river
to the ocean.

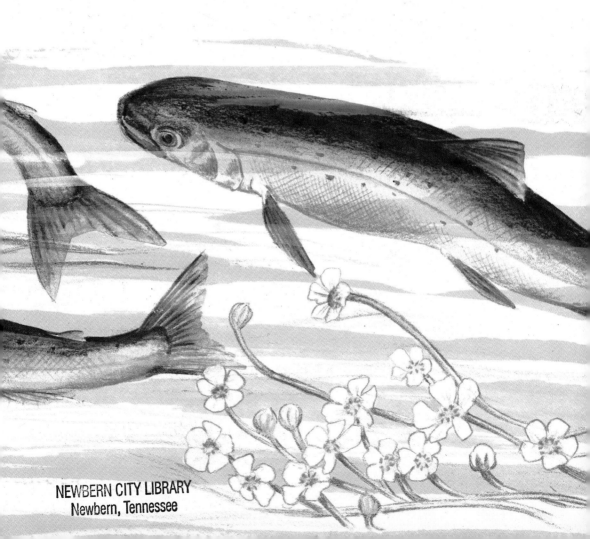

They find places where
there is plenty of food.
They grow faster now.

The salmon swim out
into the open sea,
feeding as they go.

When it is time, these salmon
will return to lay eggs in
the river where they were born.

SALMON are among the fish that migrate from saltwater to freshwater to spawn. They return to the place where they were spawned to lay their own eggs. How they do so is a puzzle to those who study them. The journey these fish make upstream may be many miles long and involve leaping up waterfalls. Where rivers have been dammed, "fish ladders" are often built to help the salmon reach their spawning grounds.

There are two large classes of salmon, the Atlantic and the Pacific, named for the oceans where they swim. They differ in an important way. The Pacific salmon die shortly after laying their eggs; the Atlantic salmon return to saltwater and may indeed spawn twice before dying.

The names of some Pacific salmon are well-known: chinook, coho, sockeye, pink and chum. Some live to be only two years old, some to six. Other fish, squid and crustaceans are their food. The chinook, the largest, is popular with sport fishers and also commercially as a food fish, as are sockeye and pink salmon. The coho is a variety that has been stocked in the Great Lakes.

Atlantic salmon, pictured here, spawn in the fall in rivers along the eastern coast of Canada, in New England rivers, and in Greenland, Iceland, and northern European countries such as Denmark, Norway, Scotland, Holland, France and Germany.

Salmon have been endangered by commercial overfishing and changes in river courses caused by damming and pollution. Solving some of these problems requires international cooperation. Certain kinds of fishing and netting are limited or not permitted, especially during the spawning season.

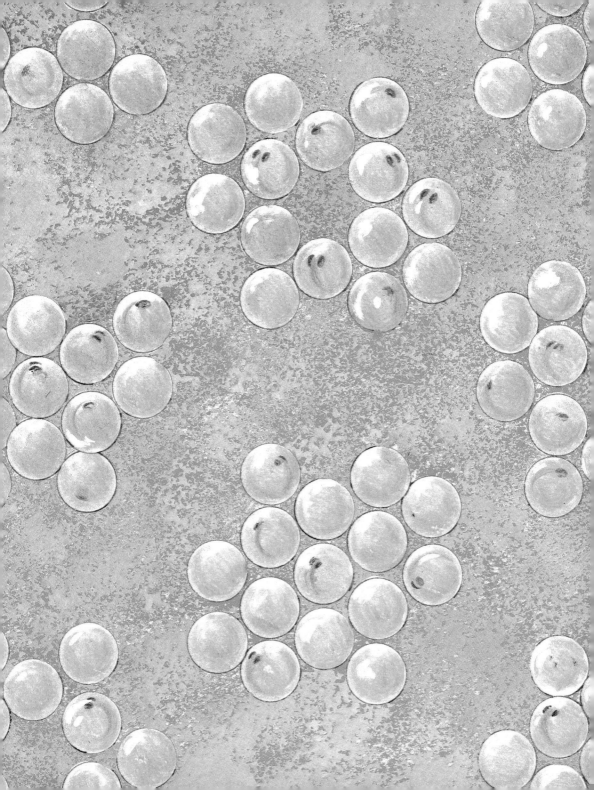

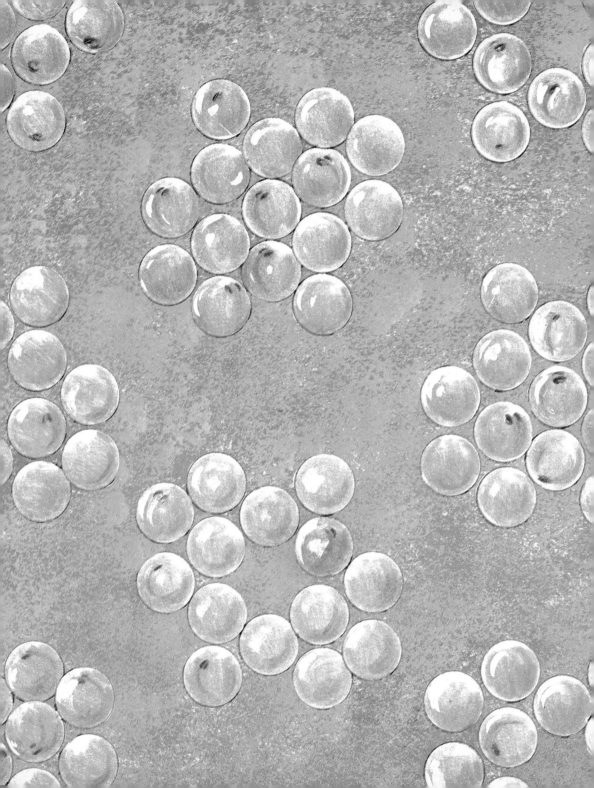